MOON LANDINGS

FIRST EDITION
Editors Kathleen Teece, Kritika Gupta; **Senior Art Editor** Jim Green; **Project Art Editor** Lucy Sims;
Art Editor Kanika Kalra; **US Editors** Jacqueline Hornberger, Allison Singer;
Jacket Coordinator Francesca Young; **Jacket Designer** Suzena Sengupta;
DTP Designers Ashok Kumar, Dheeraj Singh; **Picture Researcher** Sakshi Saluja;
Producer, Pre-Production Rob Dunn; **Senior Producer** Isabell Schart;
Managing Editors Laura Gilbert, Monica Saigal; **Managing Art Editor** Diane Peyton Jones;
Deputy Managing Art Editor Ivy Sengupta; **Delhi Team Head** Malavika Talukder;
Creative Director Helen Senior; **Publishing Director** Sarah Larter;
Reading Consultant Linda Gambrell; **Educational Consultant** Jacqueline Harris;
DK Digital Content, London Programme Manager Gareth Lowe;
Digital Producer Alex Valizadeh; **Digital Operations, Delhi Production Coordinator** Manish Bhatt

THIS EDITION
Editorial Management by Oriel Square
Produced for DK by WonderLab Group LLC
Jennifer Emmett, Erica Green, Kate Hale, *Founders*

Editors Grace Hill Smith, Libby Romero, Michaela Weglinski;
Photography Editors Kelley Miller, Annette Kiesow, Nicole DiMella; **Managing Editor** Rachel Houghton;
Designers Project Design Company; **Researcher** Michelle Harris; **Copy Editor** Lori Merritt;
Indexer Connie Binder; **Proofreader** Larry Shea; **Reading Specialist** Dr. Jennifer Albro;
Curriculum Specialist Elaine Larson

Published in the United States by DK Publishing
1745 Broadway, 20th Floor, New York, NY 10019
Copyright © 2023 Dorling Kindersley Limited
DK, a Division of Penguin Random House LLC
22 23 24 25 26 10 9 8 7 6 5 4 3 2 1
001-333982-June/2023

A catalog record for this book
is available from the Library of Congress.
HC ISBN: 9780-7440-7307-2
PB ISBN: 9780-7440-7308-9

DK books are available at special discounts when purchased in bulk for sales promotions, premiums,
fundraising, or educational use. For details, contact: DK Publishing Special Markets,
1745 Broadway, 20th Floor, New York, NY 10019
SpecialSales@dk.com

Printed and bound in China

The publisher would like to thank the following for their kind permission to reproduce their images:
a=above; c=center; b=below; l=left; r=right; t=top; b/g=background
Alamy Stock Photo: Liu Jie / Xinhua 56bl, Alejandro Miranda 59br; **Dreamstime.com:** Diego Barucco 7crb, Roblan 11cra;
Getty Images: Archive Photos / PhotoQuest 4-5, Roger Viollet 10tl; **Getty Images / iStock:** m-gucci 8tl; NASA: 17crb, 19tr, 19cr, 20tl,
21tr, 23tr, 23br, 24-25tc, 25cr, 30tl, 33br, 36bc, 40tl, 49tr, 51tr, 52t, 53tr, 55tr, 56t, 57tr, GSFC / Arizona State University 54-55b, JPL /
USGS 9cr, SLS / Terry White 57bl
Cover images: *Front and Spine:* **Shutterstock.com:** Vadim Sadovski

All other images © Dorling Kindersley
For more information see: www.dkimages.com

For the curious
www.dk.com

MOON LANDINGS

Shoshana Z. Weider

CONTENTS

Earth and its Moon

THE MOON AND SPACE TRAVEL

The Moon has fascinated people for thousands of years. It is Earth's only natural satellite, and it constantly orbits (circles) our planet.

On average, the Moon is about 240,000 miles (386,000 km) from Earth. In space distance, that is practically next door.

The Moon was important in many ancient religions. People would hold festivals when the full Moon shone at certain times during the year. The ancient Greeks believed that a moon goddess, Phoebe, dragged it into the sky each night with her chariot.

We know that the Moon is extremely ancient—about 4.5 billion years old. This is almost as old as Earth. Scientists believe the Moon formed when Earth and another body crashed into each other. The debris from the collision flew out into space. Gravity pulled it together to form the Moon.

Sizeable Moon
More than 200 moons orbit planets in our solar system. Out of all those moons, Earth's Moon is the fifth largest.

Moon Size
The Moon is about one-fourth as wide as Earth.

The Moon and Earth
It takes the Moon 27.3 days to rotate on its axis. It takes the same amount of time for the Moon to orbit Earth. That's why people on Earth always see the same side of the Moon.

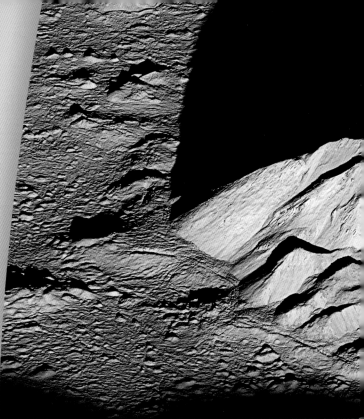

The central peak of the Moon's Tycho crater

The Moon is the brightest object we see in the night sky. Sometimes, it is even visible during the day. We only ever see one side of the Moon as it travels around Earth.

The Moon is a rocky body covered in craters and mountains. From Earth, we see darker and lighter spots. The dark areas are craters filled with a type of rock called basalt.

The lighter areas are mountains, made from a paler rock, known as anorthosite.

During the day, it is very hot on the Moon. At night, it is very cold. The Moon has no atmosphere, and there is no liquid water on its surface. No plants or animals can live on the Moon.

Lunar Landscape
The light areas on the Moon are called highlands. The dark areas are called maria, which is Latin for "seas." The dark areas are basins that were filled with lava between 3.8 and 2.8 billion years ago.

A New Purpose
The German V-2 rocket was designed as a weapon. But even its creators saw how the technology could someday take people into space.

Our journey to the Moon began when humans sent an object into space for the first time. This was a German V-2 rocket, launched on June 20, 1944. The rocket reached a height of 109 miles (175 km) above Earth. Yet this was still a huge distance from the Moon.

After World War II, many of the engineers who built the V-2 rockets moved to the USA. The rockets were soon made to be better and more powerful. Many exciting V-2 missions were carried out. In 1947, living creatures were sent into space for the first time inside a V-2. These were tiny fruit flies!

A US rocket that used parts of the V-2, Bumper 8, was launched from Cape Canaveral, Florida, in July 1950.

First Launch

Bumper 8 was the first US rocket ever launched at Cape Canaveral, Florida. By the late 1950s, Cape Canaveral had become a home to the US space program.

Fruit Flies in Space

It was no accident that fruit flies were the first creatures sent into space. Fruit flies are small, and they reproduce quickly. And, genetically speaking, fruit flies and humans are surprisingly alike. Studying fruit flies helps scientists learn how astronauts would be affected by space.

The Cold War
The struggle for superiority between the USA and the Soviet Union was called the Cold War. It lasted for nearly 50 years.

The Space Race
During the Cold War, being the first to do anything in outer space was seen as a huge victory. Space was the final frontier. People believed that the country that controlled space would prove its role as a superpower.

After 1945, there was a tense period between the USA and the Soviet Union (now Russia). The two nations began competing to be the first to send people into space. This was the start of the "Space Race."

In 1957, the Soviets were the first to put an object into orbit around Earth. This small metal satellite was called Sputnik 1. In 1959, the Soviets also landed the first robotic probe on the Moon's surface.

The Russians' next achievement was even more daring. On April 12, 1961, cosmonaut Yuri Gagarin became the first person in space. He made one orbit of Earth in the Vostok 1 spacecraft.

The world's first artificial satellite, Sputnik 1, was the size of a beach ball. It orbited Earth for three months.

Sputnik 1
"Beep, beep." Simple radio signals coming from Sputnik 1 announced the first major victory in the Space Race. People tuned in to their radios to hear the satellite's transmissions all over the world.

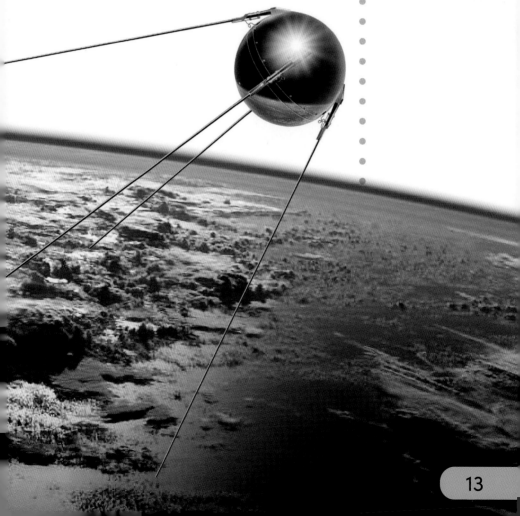

IMPORTANT FIGURES

These are some of the many scientists and engineers whose work helped to develop successful missions to the Moon.

Konstantin Tsiolkovsky

Born: 1857
Died: 1935
Nationality: Russian

Tsiolkovsky wrote one of the first books that used science and math to explain how rockets could travel to space.

Valentina Tereshkova

Born: 1937
Nationality: Russian

Originally an engineer, cosmonaut Tereshkova was the first woman to fly in space. She orbited Earth in Vostok 6, in 1963.

Wernher von Braun

Born: 1912
Died: 1977
Nationality: German

Von Braun played an important role in the design of rockets for the National Aeronautics and Space Administration (NASA), including the Saturn V vehicle for the Apollo missions.

John C. Houbolt

Born: 1919
Died: 2014
Nationality: American

Houbolt helped to plan the "lunar-orbit-rendezvous" method for landing humans on the Moon. This was used in the Apollo missions.

Robert H. Goddard

Born: 1882
Died: 1945
Nationality: American

Goddard created and launched the world's first liquid-fueled rocket. His ideas and inventions helped develop modern rockets for long-distance space flights.

GOING TO THE MOON

The US president John F. Kennedy made a bold move in May 1961. This was shortly after Alan Shepard had become the first American to go to space. Kennedy promised to land a man on the Moon and return him safely to Earth before 1970.

Project Mercury
Project Mercury, which operated from 1961 to 1963, was NASA's first human spaceflight program. It conducted 25 flights—six of which carried astronauts. Its goal was to learn if humans could survive in space.

The Gemini Program
NASA's Gemini program lasted from 1965 to 1966. These missions were used to test equipment and train astronauts and ground crew for a flight to the Moon.

President Kennedy giving his "We choose to go to the Moon" speech at Rice Stadium, Texas, in September 1962

Americans started to make new programs that would send more missions to space. These were controlled by NASA, which is the American space agency. NASA was soon sending astronauts into orbit around Earth and robotic probes to the Moon.

To land humans on the Moon, NASA created the Apollo program. However, in January 1967, there was a tragic fire during training for the first Apollo mission. It killed all three of the crew.

Alan Shepard
On May 5, 1961, Shepard became the first American in space. Inside the Freedom 7 spacecraft, he flew 116 miles (187 km) above Earth for 15 minutes, 28 seconds.

John Glenn
Flying in Friendship 7 on February 20, 1962, Glenn became the first American to orbit Earth.

Lunar Module pilot Walt Cunningham inside
the Apollo 7 Command and Service Module

Apollo 7 was the first successful crewed Apollo mission. It was launched in October 1968. Wally Schirra, Donn Eisele, and Walt Cunningham were the astronauts. They spent nearly 11 days orbiting Earth. Life inside the spacecraft was very cramped. Because there was no gravity, the astronauts could float around. However, there was little room to move or exercise.

The astronauts slept in a section of the craft called the Command and Service Module, strapped onto their couches. They also ate three freeze-dried meals there each day.

All three astronauts came down with a flu-like illness. This could have been a cold that spread between them in the tiny space!

Circling Earth
The Apollo 7 crew orbited Earth 163 times.

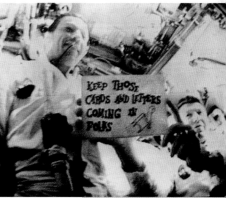

Prime Time
During the Apollo 7 mission, the crew conducted several live press conferences with reporters on Earth. This was the first live broadcast from space.

Saturn V
The Saturn V (as in Roman numeral five) rocket was as tall as a 36-story building. Fully fueled, it weighed as much as 400 elephants!

Mission Accomplished
Apollo 8 showed NASA that it now had everything it needed to safely send astronauts to the Moon and back.

Apollo 8 was the next mission. It took place during December 1968. Launched on a hugely powerful Saturn V rocket, it was the first Apollo mission to travel all the way to the Moon.

The mission's astronauts, Frank Borman, Jim Lovell, and Bill Anders, were the first humans to get far enough from Earth to see the whole sphere of our planet. They also witnessed a beautiful "earthrise" from lunar orbit.

The astronauts made an emotional television broadcast on Christmas Eve. Viewers on Earth watched in awe as the astronauts flew their spacecraft over the Moon's barren surface.

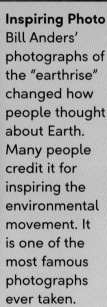

Inspiring Photo
Bill Anders' photographs of the "earthrise" changed how people thought about Earth. Many people credit it for inspiring the environmental movement. It is one of the most famous photographs ever taken.

A photograph of the "earthrise" taken by Bill Anders from Apollo 8

Apollo 9 took place in March 1969. It was the first time that the Lunar Module was tested in space. This was the part of the spacecraft that would eventually take astronauts all the way to the Moon's surface.

The Apollo 9 astronauts spent 10 days orbiting Earth. They practiced separating the Command and Service Module and the Lunar Module. The two sections of the spacecraft were flown more than 110 miles (177 km) apart and brought back together again.

During the mission, Rusty Schweickart performed a "spacewalk." He spent 37 minutes outside the spacecraft. Imagine floating in space and looking down on Earth!

Call Signs
Apollo 9 was the first mission that had call signs for the spacecraft. Crew members called the Command and Service Module *Gumdrop*. The Lunar Module was known as *Spider*.

A photograph of Dave Scott exiting the Command Module taken by astronaut Rusty Schweickart during the spacewalk

So Close...Yet So Far
Stafford and Cernan might have been able to land on the Moon. But the Lunar Module they flew was a test model. It would have been too heavy to lift off and fly back up to the Command Module.

Apollo 10 was the final rehearsal for landing people on the Moon. Astronauts Tom Stafford, John Young, and Gene Cernan lifted off on their Saturn V rocket on May 18, 1969.

Four days later, Stafford and Cernan flew the Lunar Module to within nine miles (14 km) of the lunar surface. Young stayed in the Command and Service Module orbiting the Moon.

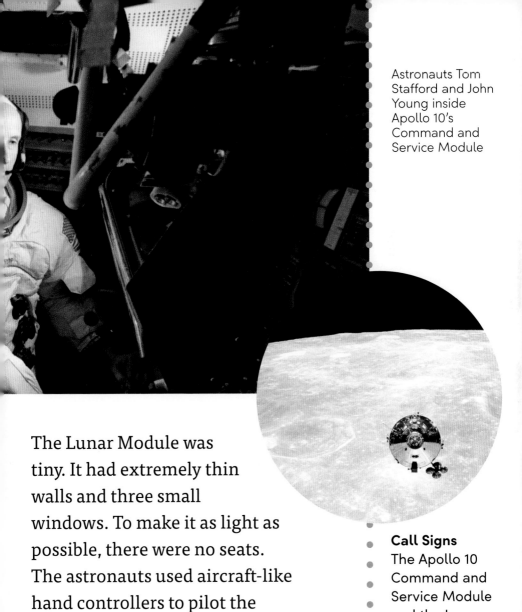

Astronauts Tom Stafford and John Young inside Apollo 10's Command and Service Module

The Lunar Module was tiny. It had extremely thin walls and three small windows. To make it as light as possible, there were no seats. The astronauts used aircraft-like hand controllers to pilot the Lunar Module.

It looked like the USA would win the Space Race, but the Soviets were also still hard at work. They continued to send probes into orbit around the Moon.

Call Signs
The Apollo 10 Command and Service Module and the Lunar Module were nicknamed *Charlie Brown* and *Snoopy*, after characters in the "Peanuts" comic strip.

Apollo Spacecraft

The spacecraft that sent astronauts to the Moon, and brought them back to Earth, were made up of several different parts. The rocket that carried them to space was called Saturn V.

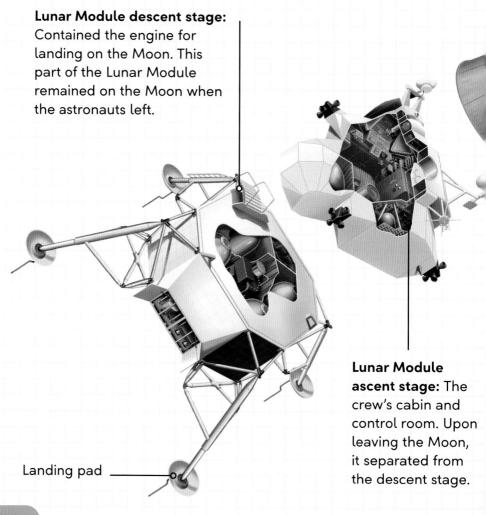

Lunar Module descent stage: Contained the engine for landing on the Moon. This part of the Lunar Module remained on the Moon when the astronauts left.

Lunar Module ascent stage: The crew's cabin and control room. Upon leaving the Moon, it separated from the descent stage.

Landing pad

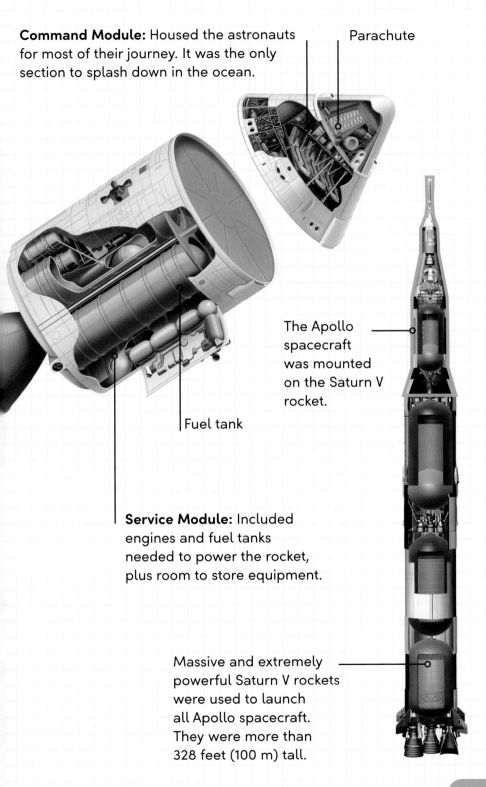

Command Module: Housed the astronauts for most of their journey. It was the only section to splash down in the ocean.

Parachute

Fuel tank

The Apollo spacecraft was mounted on the Saturn V rocket.

Service Module: Included engines and fuel tanks needed to power the rocket, plus room to store equipment.

Massive and extremely powerful Saturn V rockets were used to launch all Apollo spacecraft. They were more than 328 feet (100 m) tall.

APOLLO 11

Space Rush
The Apollo 11 mission was scheduled to lift off two months after Apollo 10's return. And it was just seven months after Apollo 8, when NASA sent its first astronauts to the Moon.

It seemed more and more likely that the US would finally land a person on the Moon. NASA had now shown that they had spacecraft good enough for a mission to the Moon's surface. They were ready to meet the challenge set by President Kennedy back in 1961.

The Apollo 11 mission was scheduled for July 1969. NASA would attempt to land people on the Moon and return them safely to Earth.

Meanwhile, the Soviets were behind in the Space Race. A massive explosion at the Soviet launch facility in July 1969 set them back even further.

The Apollo 11 mission patch was worn by the astronauts on their uniforms.

The Saturn V rocket being assembled

Silent Pursuit
The Space Race was a real competition. But the Soviet Union never officially announced its intent to land a cosmonaut, the Soviet version of an astronaut, on the Moon.

Apollo 11 was to have a three-person crew. NASA required all early astronauts to be military test pilots. They needed to be comfortable with high-risk flying. Women were disqualified from becoming astronauts because there were no female test pilots at that time.

The astronauts chosen for this mission had performed well on NASA's previous space flights. Commander Neil Armstrong would be in overall charge of the mission. He and Edwin "Buzz" Aldrin were to land on the lunar surface. Meanwhile, Michael Collins would remain in the Command and Service Module as it orbited the Moon.

Portrait of the Apollo 11 crew— Neil Armstrong (*left*), Michael Collins (*center*), and Edwin "Buzz" Aldrin (*right*)

Close Call
Armstrong had a close call during Apollo 11 training. The Lunar Landing Research Vehicle (LLRV) he was flying malfunctioned. He ejected from the vehicle seconds before it crashed.

All Apollo astronauts completed a tough training program before their missions. They needed to learn how to control the spacecraft. They practiced flying the Lunar Module by piloting the Lunar Landing Research Vehicle. The Apollo missions would end when the Command and Service Module splashed down in the ocean.

The Lunar Landing Research Vehicle was nicknamed the "flying bedstead."

To prepare the astronauts for their mission, NASA built a simulated indoor moonscape in Houston, Texas. It recreated part of the moon's surface in an Arizona crater. And the astronauts went everywhere from the Grand Canyon to Iceland to study rock formations.

The astronauts were therefore taught to survive in the water and on deserted islands.

The astronauts also studied rock types. This meant that they could examine the lunar surface and choose the best rock samples to bring back to Earth for scientific study.

Apollo 11's launch day dawned on July 16, 1969. More than one million excited people lined the beaches in Florida near the launch site. They were going to watch the start of a great adventure.

Despite having all the world watching them, the astronauts carefully completed their final tasks. They ate breakfast, put on their space suits, and made their way to the launchpad at the Kennedy Space Center. The countdown had begun.

At nine seconds before launch, Saturn V's five engines ignited. They reached full power at the moment of liftoff: time zero. The huge rocket slowly began to rise, with its roar being heard for hundreds of miles.

Former US president Lyndon B. Johnson and former first lady of the United States "Lady Bird" Johnson watching the launch of Apollo 11

Into Orbit
Apollo 11 launched on July 16, 1969, at 9:32 a.m. It took 12 minutes for the spacecraft to enter orbit around Earth.

The Saturn V rocket launching with the Apollo 11 crew on July 16, 1969

Change of Plan

The *Eagle* overflew its intended landing site and was headed for an area covered in big rocks. Armstrong switched the controls to manual mode so he could land the Lunar Module on a smoother surface.

Call Signals

Apollo 11's Command and Service Module was known as the *Columbia*. Its Lunar Module, the *Eagle*, was made famous when Armstrong announced that "the Eagle has landed."

Apollo 11 spent two hours orbiting Earth. It was then sent on its four-day journey to the Moon. It entered lunar orbit at about 62 miles (100 km) above the surface.

The next day, Armstrong and Aldrin entered the *Eagle*. This was Apollo 11's Lunar Module. They set off on a nerve-racking descent to the lunar surface. Finally, they found a safe landing spot and touched down in a huge crater called the Sea of Tranquility—with just 45 seconds of landing fuel left!

A few hours later, Armstrong stepped onto the Moon. Millions of people watched on television as he famously said, "That's one small step for man, one giant leap for mankind." Aldrin followed, describing the empty scene as "magnificent desolation."

Buzz Aldrin climbing down the Lunar Module steps to the lunar surface

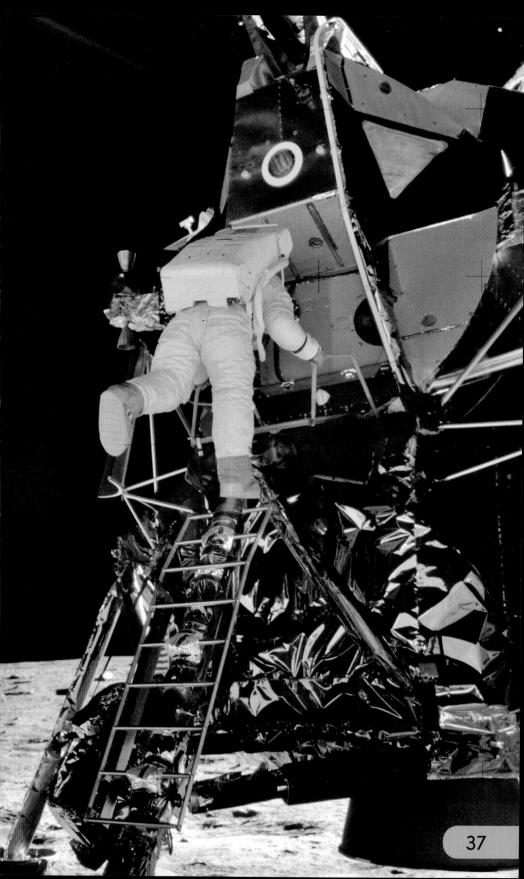

Armstrong and Aldrin walked on the Moon for more than two hours. They collected rocks and set up scientific equipment to examine the Moon's surface and interior. They also planted the US flag in the lunar soil. All too soon, it was time to reenter the *Eagle*. After resting, the two astronauts flew the craft back to the Command and Service Module.

The Flag
The Moon has no wind and virtually no atmosphere. The flag on the Moon was attached with a horizontal beam. This made the flag look like it was waving and kept it from drooping.

The historic mission ended on July 24, 1969, as the spacecraft returned to Earth. It passed safely through Earth's atmosphere. Parachutes were then deployed, before the Command and Service Module softly splashed down into the Pacific Ocean.

Lunar Plaque
The Apollo 11 astronauts left a plaque on the base of their Lunar Module to commemorate the historic nature of their expedition.

Astronaut Buzz Aldrin on the Moon with the US flag

Safe Returns
Before leaving the Command Module, the astronauts had to put on special suits—just in case they brought back Moon germs! They were also sprayed with disinfectant. Then, they boarded a raft, and a helicopter took them to the USS *Hornet*.

A US Navy ship called the *Hornet* collected the astronauts. They were kept away from other people in case they had brought back diseases from the Moon. US president Richard Nixon welcomed and congratulated them through a glass window. Meanwhile, people around the world joyfully celebrated the successful mission.

The astronauts were in isolation for three weeks. Afterward, they could finally join the parties being thrown in their honor. They took part in parades around the USA, and each astronaut was awarded the Presidential Medal of Freedom. They also received international praise during their 45-day tour of 25 foreign countries.

The Apollo 11 astronauts inside the Mobile Quarantine Facility on the *Hornet*, as president Nixon welcomes them back to Earth on July 24, 1969

ORNET + 3

Women of Apollo

NASA banned women from becoming astronauts until 1983. But women have always played important roles in getting missions off the ground and to the Moon.

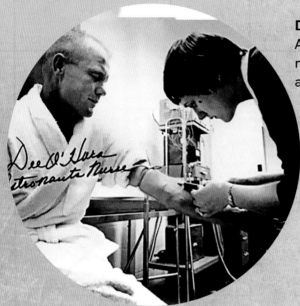

Dee O'Hara
At NASA, O'Hara was the nurse for all the Apollo astronauts.

Margaret Hamilton
Hamilton led the team that developed the in-flight software for the spacecraft.

Billie Robertson
Robertson was a mathematician for NASA. She helped develop computer programs for the Apollo launches.

Poppy Northcutt
Northcutt was the first female engineer to work in NASA's Mission Control.

Katherine Johnson
A brilliant mathematician, Johnson helped figure out the trajectory, or path, of the spacecraft. Her work was critical to several NASA missions.

AFTER THE FIRST LANDING

Humans had finally landed on the Moon, but there was still a lot more to do up there! More Apollo missions were planned. Apollo 12 flew to the Moon again in November 1969.

Pete Conrad and Alan Bean landed their Lunar Module in an area called the Ocean of Storms. They collected part of a probe that had been flown to the Moon in 1967. Scientists wanted to see how it had changed in space.

Some photographs taken by the astronauts on the Moon were lost because Bean accidentally left some of the film there! He later became an artist. He used paint containing Moon dust to draw lunar scenes.

Lightning Strike
About 37 seconds after it launched, the Saturn V rocket carrying Apollo 12 was struck by lightning. Twenty seconds later, another bolt hit the rocket, knocking some of the spacecraft's systems off-line. Luckily, flight operations were able to get everything working again so the mission could continue.

The Apollo 12 crew— Alan Bean (*left*), Richard Gordon (*center*), and Pete Conrad (*right*)

Apollo 13's Jim Lovell, Jack Swigert, and Fred Haise on the USS *Iwo Jima* after safely splashing down in the South Pacific Ocean

Apollo 13 Lifeline
Before Apollo 11's flight to the Moon, Johnson plotted backup navigation charts. Astronauts could use the charts if a spacecraft's electronics failed. Her work helped save the Apollo 13 astronauts.

Apollo 13 lifted off from Florida on April 11, 1970. It carried astronauts Jim Lovell, Jack Swigert, and Fred Haise. Almost 56 hours into their journey to the Moon, however, an explosion happened on board. This caused the spacecraft to quickly lose oxygen and power.

NASA engineers on Earth had to rapidly plan a rescue mission. They told the astronauts to use the Lunar Module as a lifeboat. The astronauts found their way home by using the position of the stars as a guide. This was a backup method masterminded by mathematician Katherine Johnson. The crew safely splashed down in the South Pacific on April 17.

Abort!
Apollo 13 was the only Apollo mission to be stopped midway through the flight. The crew's safe return to Earth is still considered to be Mission Control's finest hour.

NASA did not want another explosion on a spacecraft. They made improvements to the Apollo spacecraft and delayed the launch of Apollo 14 until January 31, 1971.

The Apollo 14 mission was led by Alan Shepard. He had just recovered from an illness that had almost ended his career. Alan Shepard and Edgar Mitchell stayed on the lunar surface for more than 33 hours. Stuart Roosa remained orbiting the Moon in the Command and Service Module. Shepard and Mitchell explored the Fra Mauro region of the Moon. They collected rock samples and carried out scientific experiments. Shepard even found time to play some golf!

Moon Trees
The Apollo 14 astronauts took a canister of tree seeds on their mission. They studied the effects of deep space on the seeds. Upon the astronauts' return, the seeds were germinated and planted all around the world.

Astronaut Alan Shepard assembling scientific equipment on the Moon

Playing It Safe

Apollo 15's lunar rover had a range of 40 miles (64 km), but the astronauts were only allowed to travel three miles (4.8 km) from the Lunar Module. If the rover broke down, they needed to be close enough to walk back!

Apollo 15 was the first in a series of missions designed to stay on the lunar surface for a longer amount of time. Apollo 15 carried a lunar rover to the Moon for the first time. The astronauts could explore a much larger area with this vehicle.

Astronaut James Irwin saluting the US flag during the moonwalk

Dave Scott and James Irwin landed near a deep valley, called Hadley Rille, on July 30, 1971. They collected 170 pounds (77 kg) of lunar rocks to bring home. This was much more than from previous missions. The Command and Service Module also carried instruments that studied the lunar surface from orbit.

Ancient Rocks
One of the rocks Apollo 15 astronauts brought back was determined to be about four billion years old. It was nicknamed the "Genesis Rock." Even older rocks were found on other missions.

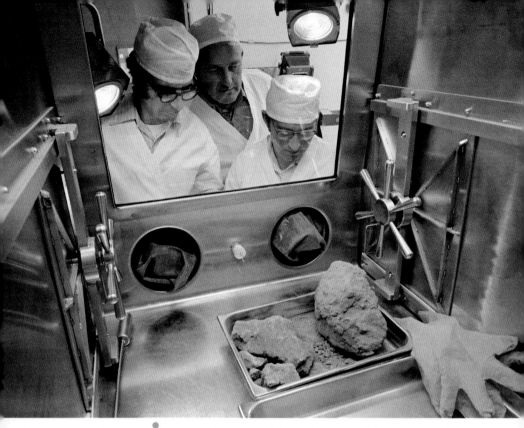

Lunar Surprise
Scientists thought highlands on the Moon were the result of volcanic eruptions. So, Apollo 16 astronauts searched for volcanic rocks. They didn't find any. The rocks they did find, however, showed how meteors striking the Moon's surface had formed the hills.

Specialists studying a lunar rock brought back by the Apollo 16 astronauts at the Lunar Receiving Laboratory. This rock is popularly known as "Big Muley."

The last missions to land on the Moon were Apollo 16 and 17 in 1972. Apollo 16's John Young and Charles Duke explored a mountainous area of the Moon. They collected the largest lunar rock sample ever. It weighed almost 26 pounds (12 kg).

On the way to the Moon, the Apollo 17 crew snapped a beautiful photograph of the entire Earth.

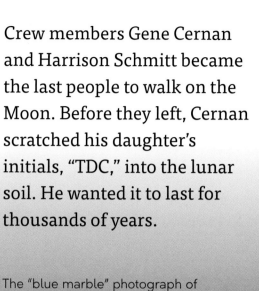

Crew members Gene Cernan and Harrison Schmitt became the last people to walk on the Moon. Before they left, Cernan scratched his daughter's initials, "TDC," into the lunar soil. He wanted it to last for thousands of years.

The "blue marble" photograph of Earth taken by the Apollo 17 crew

Farewell, Moon
Apollo 17 was the last of the Apollo missions. The astronauts left a plaque on the base of their Lunar Module, which they left on the moon, to commemorate the end of the program.

Mapping the Moon

The Lunar Reconnaissance Orbiter's (LRO) primary mission was to create a complete map of resources and features found on the Moon.

There has been no human exploration of the Moon since the Apollo program ended. It costs a huge amount of money to send people there. However, scientists from around the world continue to study the Moon. They use data and samples taken by Apollo spacecraft, rovers, and lunar satellites.

NASA's uncrewed Lunar Reconnaissance Orbiter was launched on June 18, 2009, and it still orbits the Moon today. It studies the Moon in great detail. Its findings are helping scientists and engineers to plan future lunar landings. If all goes to plan, that could happen in the next few years.

LRO Discovery
Among the LRO's many findings is evidence of water ice at the Moon's south pole.

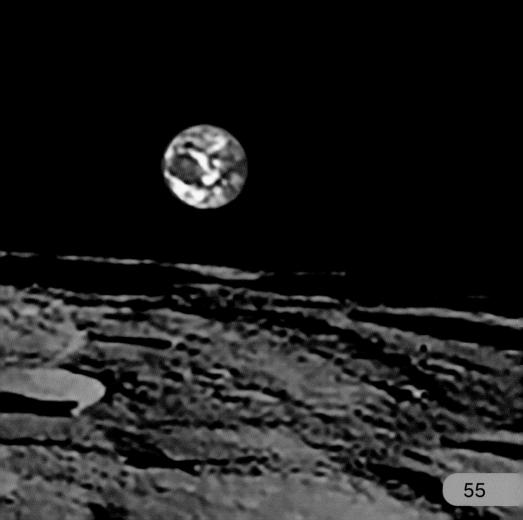

Introducing the xEMU
NASA designers have created a new spacesuit for the upcoming missions to the Moon. Called the xEMU (Exploration Extravehicular Mobility Unit), it is more flexible, versatile, and durable than spacesuits used in the past.

NASA's next big venture is called the Artemis program. In cooperation with several other countries and private corporations, the space agency plans to return humans to the Moon very soon.

Astronauts will board a new spacecraft called the Orion. A massive new rocket called the Space Launch System will launch them into lunar orbit. Once in space, the Orion will dock at the Gateway, an outpost orbiting the Moon.

NASA's Orion spacecraft is built to take humans farther than they've ever gone before.

From here, astronauts will travel back and forth to the Moon. Over time, they will build a permanent base at the Moon's south pole. This base will be a stepping stone to the next goal...sending humans to Mars. Who knows? Maybe you could go to the Moon or Mars someday!

Survival Suits
During Artemis missions, astronauts will wear Orion Crew Survival System spacesuits. The flight suits will protect astronauts during launch, reentry, and emergency situations. Even the suit's color has a purpose. Bright orange makes it easy for rescuers to find astronauts in the ocean if they need to exit Orion before emergency personnel arrive.

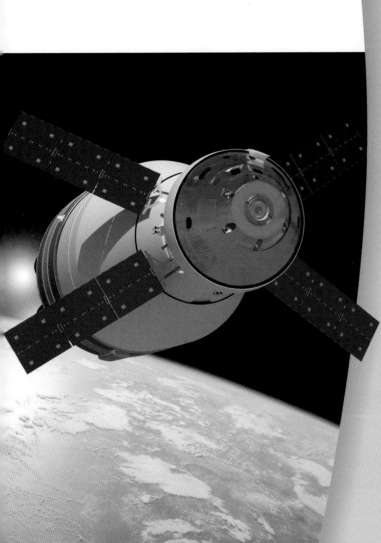

Lunar Rovers

Several crewed and robotic vehicles have driven around on the lunar surface to aid scientific studies of the Moon.

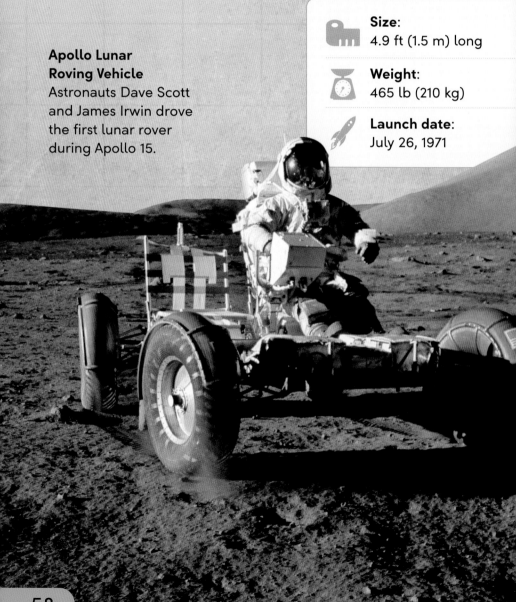

Apollo Lunar Roving Vehicle
Astronauts Dave Scott and James Irwin drove the first lunar rover during Apollo 15.

Size:
4.9 ft (1.5 m) long

Weight:
465 lb (210 kg)

Launch date:
July 26, 1971

Lunokhod 2

Part of the Luna 21 mission, this was the Soviet Union's second robotic rover.

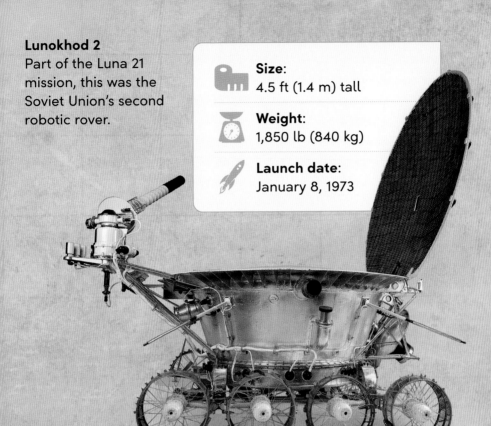

Size:
4.5 ft (1.4 m) tall

Weight:
1,850 lb (840 kg)

Launch date:
January 8, 1973

Yutu 2

This Chinese rover, part of the Chang'e 4 mission, was the first rover to land on the far side of the Moon.

 Size:
4.9 ft (1.5 m) tall

 Weight:
310 lb (140 kg)

 Launch date:
December 1, 2013

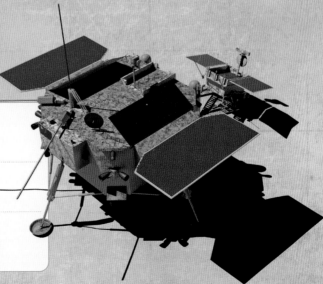

INTERNATIONAL MOON EXPLORATIONS

In recent decades, space agencies from around the world have sent probes to orbit the Moon.

SMART-1 (2003–2006)
The aim of the European Space Agency's SMART–1 satellite was to demonstrate new instrument technologies rather than make scientific discoveries.

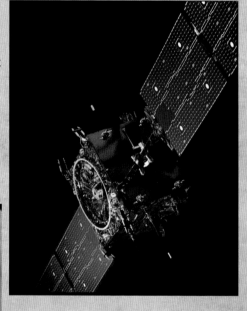

Chang'e 1 (2007–2009)
The Chang'e 1 satellite, named after the Chinese lunar goddess, was the first phase of the Chinese Lunar Exploration Program.

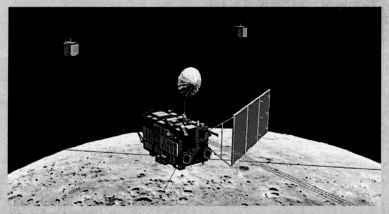

SELENE (2007–2009)
This was the second probe sent to the Moon by Japan.
It was nicknamed *Kaguya* and provided detailed maps
of the Moon.

**Chandrayaan-1
(2008–2009)**
Results from the
Indian Space Research
Organisation's first
lunar satellite led to
the discovery of water
in the Moon's soil.

GLOSSARY

Apollo
The US space agency program tasked with sending a human to the Moon

Astronaut
Someone who has trained to fly a spacecraft and work in space

Data
Information often involving numbers, such as measurements of distance

Earthrise
The view of Earth rising above the horizon from the Moon

Engine
The part of a craft that provides power for it to move

Lunar
Related to the Moon

Module
A part of a spacecraft

Moon
A natural satellite orbiting Earth

NASA
The US agency in charge of missions to space—short for National Aeronautics and Space Administration

Orbit
To move in a circle around something

Probe
An uncrewed spacecraft that sends information about space back to Earth

Rocket
A missile or craft that uses an engine to fly

Satellite
An object that orbits another

Software
Programs on a computer that tell it how to perform tasks

Spacecraft
A vehicle or robotic machine designed to fly through space

Space Race
The competition between the US and the Soviet Union to put a human on the Moon

Splashdown
When a spacecraft lands in the ocean after returning to Earth

INDEX

 QUIZ

Answer the questions to see what you have learned. Check your answers in the key below.

1. How old is the Moon?

2. Where is basalt rock found on the Moon?

3. Which president famously promised to land a man on the Moon?

4. In which year did Apollo 11 launch?

5. Who was the first person to set foot on the Moon?

6. Who was the first female engineer at NASA Mission Control?

7. What was China's rover Yutu 2 the first rover to do?

8. What is the name of NASA's program that will take humans back to the Moon?

1. About 4.5 billion years old 2. Craters 3. John F. Kennedy
4. 1969 5. Neil Armstrong 6. Poppy Northcutt
7. Land on the far side of the Moon 8. Artemis